TENNESSEE

A Picture Book to Remember Her By

CRESCENT BOOKS
NEW YORK

CLB 1776
©1987 Colour Library Books Ltd., Guildford, Surrey, England.
Printed and bound in Barcelona, Spain by Cronion, S.A.
1987 edition published by Crescent Books, distributed by Crown Publishers, Inc.
ISBN 0 517 644126
hgfedcba

It's the home of Elvis Presley and the birthplace of the Grand Ole Opry, of Davy Crockett and Sam Houston. It extends from the heights of the Smoky Mountains to the bottomlands of the Mississippi River. It's a place where some people live vey much like their predecessors who fought the Cherokee and Chickasaw Indians for their farms, and where nuclear physicists have found a nice place to live.

Much of Tennessee didn't come into the 20th century until the century was three decades old and the Federal Government began building hydroelectric projects in the Valley of the Tennessee River. Though seven states share the benefits of the Tennessee Valley Authority, Tennessee is the major beneficiary of the program that provides low-cost electricity for rural areas and industrial centers as well as flood control, land conservation and river navigation.

TVA united the states it serves, but it also united Tennessee itself. In a way. Because the state is divided from north to south by mountains and valleys into three distinct regions, the only groups that were ever united before were the Middle and West, and that was a fragile union at best. The people in the West, who sided with the South in the War Between the States, are as different from East Tennesseans, who fought with the North in the War, as an Appalachian farmer is from a Mississippi planter. Some people in the eastern mountains still regard West Tennessee as a worthless swamp; some in the Middle section, where they raise fine horses and rich tobacco, think both East and West lean too far North. It's hard to forget the Civil War in Tennessee. There are reminders everywhere in places with names like Chickamauga, Shiloh, Chattanooga and Nashville. More than 600 major battles were fought in Tennessee, some of the bloodiest of the War.

In the years before the War, Tennessee was thought of as the wild frontier, personified by one of its famous sons, President Andrew Jackson. It was he who ended the short tradition that politics were best left in the hands of an aristocracy, and not only encouraged common people to participate in the political process, but convinced many that their own destiny, like his, was linked to taming the Western wilderness.

After the Civil War, the state settled down to growing cotton and never really got back into the mainstream of American life until TVA was established. Today, people who call Nashville the "Wall Street of the South" mean what they say, and the city has gotten so cosmopolitan that many wonder if it still has a legitimate claim to its other title of America's country music capital. And though the blues were developed in Memphis, they're not singing the blues there these days, either. Business is good and getting better. In fact, the whole state is on the move. And the direction is up.

Facing page: a mural in Memphis, reflecting the city's musical heritage.

Memphis. (Right, below, bottom left and bottom right) the Mid American Plaza; (center right) River Walk; (facing page and overleaf right) Mud Island and (overleaf left) the Wolf River.

Memphis. Facing page: (top left) statue of Elvis Presley; (top right) Court Square; (bottom left) the Court House and (bottom right) the Botanical Gardens. This page: (top left) a building on 3rd Street; (top right) Mid American Plaza and (above) the Court House. Center left: the Administrative Building and (left) the Jones Hall, both at the State University.

Memphis. Above: the Memphis
Pink Palace Museum, which
traces the history of the
region from the days of the
dinosaurs to the present
day. Right: an excursion
boat on the Wolf River.
Below: the reconstructed
interior of an 1870s
steamboat in the River
Museum. Far right: the city
from Mud Island.

Memphis. Far left bottom, far left center, far left top and top center: Beale Street. Left, above, top right and center: Libertyland, which lies in the Mid South Fair Grounds on Central Avenue. Overleaf: (left) Beale Street and (right) River Walk.

Memphis. Above: the bridge to Mud Island. Right and above right: the River Walk and (top left) log rolling, all on Mud Island. Bottom right: the Chucalissa Indian Village. Remaining pictures: The Memphis Zoological Gardens and Aquarium.

Memphis. Left: Magevney
House. Bottom center:
Wolf River. Far left:
stained-glass in the
Mallory-Neely House. Top
left: Dixon Gallery and
Gardens. Remaining
pictures: the Victorian
Village District.

Left: an antique-style restaurant in the old railway town of Jackson. Below: the reconstructed home of David Crockett at Rutherford, which shows the simple life of a frontiersman in the early 19th century. Bottom: a roadsign indicating the location of David Crockett's home.

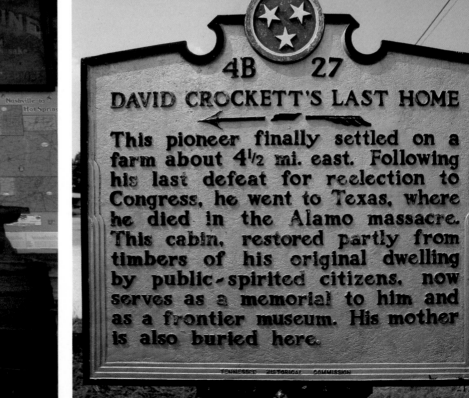

4B 27

DAVID CROCKETT'S LAST HOME

This pioneer finally settled on a farm about 4½ mi. east. Following his last defeat for reelection to Congress, he went to Texas, where he died in the Alamo massacre. This cabin, restored partly from timbers of his original dwelling by public-spirited citizens, now serves as a memorial to him and as a frontier museum. His mother is also buried here.

TENNESSEE HISTORICAL COMMISSION

Right: the bridge across the Tennessee at Paris Landing. Remaining pictures: scenes at Fort Donelson National Military Park, where General Grant defeated a Confederate force under General Buckner.

Right, below, bottom left and below right: Clarksville, named for the Revolutionary War officer, General George Rogers Clark. Bottom right: a view from the L&C Building, (facing page top) Deaderick Street and (facing page bottom) 5th Avenue, all in Nashville.

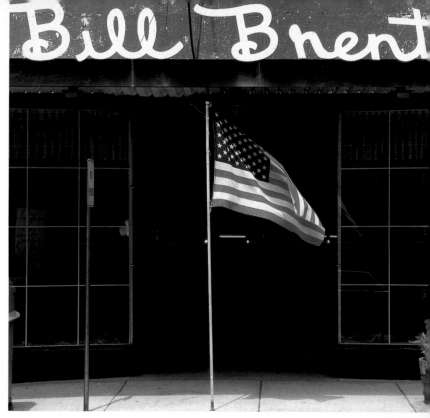

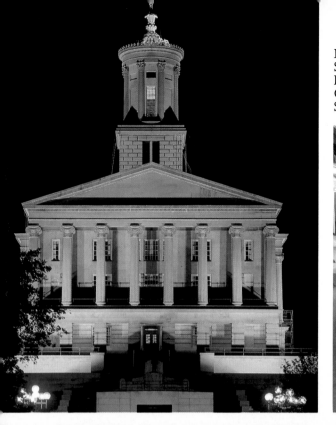

Nashville. Facing page and bottom: Deaderick Street and the columns of the War Memorial Building. Below: an exhibit from the Car Collectors Hall of Fame. Left: the fine Doric State Capitol which was completed in 1859.

Nashville. Top and right: the State Capitol.
Above: the War Memorial Building. Facing page:
(bottom) the Country Music Hall of Fame; (center
right) the Municipal Auditorium and (top left
and top right) the downtown area.

Nashville. Left: the Parthenon in Centennial Park. Top: Cheekwood. Above: the tomb of Andrew Jackson at The Hermitage. Facing page: the Jackson statue outside the Capitol.

JACKSON.

Facing page: the colorful shops along Music Row. Left: a performance at the Opryland Theater by the Lake. Below: the Car Collectors Hall of Fame. Bottom: the Encore Theater at Opryland, an entertainments complex where country music is combined with exciting rides.

Facing page: (top left) a log cabin and
(top right) Springhouse, both at The
Hermitage; (center left) Belle Meade and
(bottom) Fort Nashborough. This page:
Opryland USA, Nashville. Overleaf: (left)
Stones River National Battlefield and
(right) Burgess Falls.

Below: the Old School and (bottom left and bottom right) Christ Church, both in Rugby. Bottom center and top right: the Tennessee Technical University in Cookeville. Right and center: the Hughes Public Library, Rugby.

Pinnacle Overlook Terrace—Elevation 2,440 ft.

From this viewpoint you can look down on three states (Kentucky, Tennessee, and Virginia). More importantly, you can see the rugged terrain that the pioneers crossed on their journey west to Kentucky.

Above and facing page bottom right: Abraham Lincoln Museum, Harrogate. Left: Pinnacle Overlook. Top: La Follette. Remaining pictures: Colditz Cove State Natural Area.

41

Above, right and top center: Bristol Caverns. Top left: Cudjo Caverns. Top right: Bristol. Far right center: Fort Watauga. Remaining pictures: Rocky Mount, built in 1770.

Jonesboro (these pages) is the oldest town in Tennessee, having been chartered in 1779 when the area was part of North Carolina.

Above and top left: views from Morton
Overlook, (top right) Chimney Tops Trail
and (right) view from Little River Road,
Great Smoky Mountains National Park.
Overleaf: Gatlinburg from Crockett
Mountain.

TRADING
POST

FARMERS
DAUGHTER
Family Restaurant

Colonial
House

CAM

R

PLATE
M
BS

RIVERSIDE
PARK

WAX

Gatlinburg (above and below) is one of the most
popular resorts in the Tennessee mountains, its
success illustrated by the fact that this town of
3,000 has 23,000 beds in its varous hotels and
motels. Left: the bright lights of Pigeon Forge,
a somewhat smaller town just to the north of
Gatlinburg.

Below and right: Cable Mill and (above) the Gregg-Cable House, both in Cades Cove. This isolated mountain village is now part of Great Smoky Mountains National Park. Facing page: the Old Mill at Pigeon Forge.

Center far left: the American Museum of Science and Energy at Oak Ridge. Remaining pictures: Knoxville; (below) the William Blount House of 1792 and (top left and bottom left) James White's Fort of 1786.

CITY COUNTY BUILDING

Chattanooga. Previous pages:
(left) downtown and (right)
Boynton Park. Top left:
Georgia Avenue. Top center:
Court House. Top right:
National Cemetery. Above, left
and far left: Cravens House.
Center left: a memorial to the
Battle of Chattanooga.

Right, top and far right: a locomotive of the Tennessee Valley Railroad Museum. Above: the Chattanooga Choo Choo Complex.

Bottom left: natural bridge at Sewanee. Top left: the ancestral home of President James Polk in Columbia. Above: University of the South, Sewanee. Remaining pictures: the battlefield at Shiloh, now a National Military Park, where fierce fighting raged in April 1862. Overleaf: Pickwick Landing.

OHIO

1 2 3

BATTALIONS

6TH CAVALRY
COMMANDED BY
COL. WM. H. H. TAYLOR
1ST AND 2D BATTALIONS, HURLBUT'S (4TH) DIVISION
2D BATTALION, L. WALLACE'S (3D) DIVISION
ARMY OF THE TENNESSEE